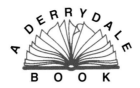

A DERRYDALE BOOK

BIG BEAR
HAS A BIRTHDAY

Written by Stephanie Laslett

Illustrated by John Blackman

Derrydale Books
New York • Avenel

Big Bear is excited.
Soon it will be his
birthday.

Today it is Monday. When is Big Bear's birthday?

Monday
Tuesday
Wednesday
Thursday
Friday
Saturday
MY BIRTHDAY (Sunday)

Not **Tuesday**. Not **Wednesday**.
Not **Thursday**. Not **Friday**.
Not **Saturday**.

It is on **Sunday**.
A whole **week** away!

Monday

Tuesday

Wednesday

Thursday

Friday

Saturday

Sunday

MY BIRTHDAY

Big Bear is having a birthday party.

Will he have it
in the **morning**? No!

Will he have it in the **afternoon**? Yes?

The **days** pass by.
Tuesday.
Wednesday.
Thursday.
Friday.
Saturday.
Soon it will
be **Sunday**!

Monday
Tuesday
Wednesday
Thursday
Friday
Saturday
MY BIRTHDAY Sunday

Hurray! **Today** is **Sunday**. It is Big Bear's birthday at last.

He puts on
his party
clothes.

But Big Bear cannot start his party yet. He has to wait for his guests to arrive.

How long will that be? Big Bear asks, looking at the clock.

His friend Morris Mouse explains. Every **day** is made up of **hours**.

Every **hour** is made up of **minutes**. And every **minute** is made up of **seconds**.

Your party will start at **12 o'clock**. It is now only **10 o'clock**.

You must wait **2 hours** for your guests to arrive.

Hurray! It is **12 o'clock** at last.

Time for the party to start.

What happens at Big Bear's party?

At **12 o'clock** Big Bear opens his presents.

At **1 o'clock** it is time for a birthday lunch.

At **4 o'clock** it is time to play blindman's buff.

At **5 o'clock** it is time to eat candy and ice cream.

At **2 o'clock** it is time to play pass-the-parcel.

At **3 o'clock** it is time to play hide-and-seek.

At **6 o'clock** it is time to go home.

Happy Birthday Big Bear!

Big Bear is
sleepy.
What time
is it now
Big Bear?

Why, **bedtime** of course.

This 1995 edition published by Derrydale Books,
distributed by Random House Value Publishing, Inc.,
40 Engelhard Avenue, Avenel, New Jersey 07001.

Random House
New York • Toronto • London • Sydney • Auckland

Produced by The Templar Company plc

Designed by Janie Louise Hunt

Printed and bound in Italy

ISBN 0-517-13996-0